Mama Yetta
and Other Poems

many strong and soon
these seeds open wings
float down parachutes
then try one more again

> – Harryette Mullen
> *Muse & Drudge*

Mama Yetta
and Other Poems

HERMINE PINSON

San Antonio, Texas
1999

Mama Yetta and Other Poems © 1999 by Hermine Pinson

First printing

ISBN: 0-930324-39-0

Wings Press
627 E. Guenther
San Antonio, Texas 78210
(210) 271-7805

On-line catalogue and ordering:
www.wingspress.com

> Except for fair use in reviews and/or scholarly considerations, no portion of this book may be reproduced without the written permission of the author.

Thanks to the Yaddo Colony, the Macdowell Colony, and the Vermont Studio Center, where some of these poems were written.

Thanks also to my publisher, Bryce Milligan, for his commitment to this project. Thanks to Dan Gutwein, who set portions of "Southland" to music, with, I must admit, some funky elegance. And to Joanne Braxton who kindly commented on stuff that needed to be commented on.

"Southland" was previously published in *Verse*. "Left-handed Poem" and "Daddy Poem" were previously published in *Sage*. "What can you do with a fan?" was previously published in *African American Review*. "From one music lover to another" was previously published in *BlondeonBlonde*. "Nina or somethin like happy" was previously published in *The Griot*. "All-Around Vampires" was previously published in *Callaloo*.

Contents

Hermine Dolore(s)z, 1998	3
Left-Handed Poem	4
Stanley	6
centrifugal force or what can you do with a fan?	8
C.C. Rider	10
All-Around Vampires	12
amateur night at the Apollo	15
Geraldine's rules of order	17
a dog's life	18
from one music lover to another	20
declaratives	22
Southland	23
28 degrees on channel 13	28
from beaumont to benin	30
Texas Poem	32
Nina or somethin like happy	33
Daddy Poem	37
indigo bunting	44
for leah	47
Yetta Yetta Yetta Yetta	49

*dedicated to
Enid Melinda*

Mama Yetta
and Other Poems

And who will join this standing up
and the ones who stood without sweet company
will sing and sing
back into the mountains and
if necessary
even under the sea

— June Jordan
Poem for South African Women

the young flesh has no creases of memory
only the scars and hardness of imitation
all of the imitation of the final wounds
runs like real blood from real flesh
even ghosts are faked out and weep.

— Thulani Davis
all the renegade ghosts rise

Hermine Dolore(s)z, 1998
b. July 20, 1953

enid's and bobby's ooh blah dee child
nineteen sixty-eight's pubescent sieve
changed her name
to elude presbyterian providence
sharpened her cheekbone blades
stretched out for the long run.
find her where dandelion dreams medusa.

Left-Handed Poem

Left hand turns inward
then rises like an ominous
hump from the limp neck
of the wrist
when I am making a point
or begging
        to differ
fingers and thumb poised
to pick up some subtle thing
            beyond themselves
came out of the womb that way
left hand turned inward
hard against the heart
transparent knuckles
but workers' hands
        like Papa Johnny's
came out that way and
        almost broke my arm
the doctor pushed me back in again
so I could come out
right
in sleep the back of the hand
is half-closed against
                the sheets
tending a dreamer's chores or
guarding against
some slight
imagined or otherwise

I used to play saxophone
Now I press fingers to soundless keys
the task:
    reach through the space on the page
for some subtle thing
half-turning motion of pincers
    in the ocean of heartways –
at rest the left hand lies:
    a failed balletic exercise
an invalid's carelessness
a pulse
a time signature
    a womb's knowledge
of life's ceaseless motion.

Stanley

Like when Stanley Turner
would line up his combat boots
with the curb
the dull leather tip
would have to be
just on the edge

he'd stand there
for hours
on this end
of his own haven
come rain or the rest

at the edge of the curb
impervious to exhaust fumes
uncalculated curses
octopus salad
bystanders
he knew a word or two
himself

Stanley expected no favors
from those who walked with purpose
up and down the street
in and out of doors
even the heat of a sun
would slow the beat of feet
on pavement

there he stood
Stanley
cursing
wobbly spittle
filled his mouth
at the corners
his hyena mouth laughing
fit to cry
for high heels and low

centrifugal force or what can you do with a fan?

      This thing will cut you   if you stick your fingers
thoughtlessly into it
        (he moved it and placed it so
        until it was catty-cornered to me)
it whirs on in the silence of the gray-walled room,
sending air through its square vents to cool
        (he turned the plastic knob on medium-high to cool
        the inside of his long ribbed thighs)

the only other sound   the only other sound
is his voice   oozy brown syrup-blues
like big joe turner   or some man
ma rainey left way back   in itta bena, mississippi
when he tried   to hold her too tight
his hot breath   on her retreating back

this thing will cool you   if you lie, sit, stand still
and smell   the dry salt on your face
if you do not reach out   to touch it

this thing will call to mind the man who danced it
into this position, still, moving, still moving
but moving in distracting circles that will cut you
into pieces if you stick your fingers thoughts
fully into it

gray blades do not roll but spin
but follow each other insistent circles
pushing air out of the center of the whirring

and will not stop for error's wayward children
will send them back into their mother's mouth
to bleed
(He turned it up high-high and stood naked
to let the air spiral his striated thighs
and he could think of serious things
like other men, women, other women, water, sunlight
fanning out in wider circles into the gray space
of the walled room
he cut it off   and no air moved
no air went any where   to cool anything
the thing sat there   in space
still
to touch

C.C. Rider

Down the winding road,
and feinting to the right
I find you conjuring mornings,
but where did you stay last night?

Midnight's hoodoo dancer
teaches demons the physics of flight
but your body enfolds little darknesses
down the winding road
and feinting to the right.

Say you'll carry me up and up
to Jicarilla's height?
While I slowburn in your Hades,
where did you stay last night?

Say you'll teach me helium steps,
to dance me to the light.
Elegbara shoes steal my pirouettes
down the winding road
and feinting to the right.

You tuck lies behind your teeth
to avert our impending fight
Answer me honestly, villain.
Where did you stay last night?

And do you still retreat from
confession's potential blight?
Deceit suits your backsliding wingtips
down the winding road
and feinting to the right.
Where did you stay last night?

All-Around Vampires

Mornings we read in the paper
a vampire has done away with
some body again
Yesterday it was a two-year-old
who just wanted to come inside
because it was dark outside
who just wanted to come inside
he didn't know the vampire would
dot his other eye
again with the bed slat
he saw no plan
lived moment to moment in his daddy's hell

he wanted to come inside the house
to flee the darkness
the promise of flies
it was a moonless night but
vampires come out in daylight too
have tv shows
shop at Bergdorf's the flea market
Pop's Greasy Barbecue
hold down nine-to-fives
three-to-elevens
eleven-to-sevens
wait tables suckle babies
chair boards

and when Oral Roberts' disciple
heavily powdered and doomed
threatens apocalypse
in soundbites
even vampires channel-surf
for the perfume of meat
Texas Chain Saw Murders
or gangsters snorting coke
off of table tops
beats weight-loss machines
on the other channel
for speed

vampires face up to ugliness
actually
mixed well
with remy martin
and beluga caviar

Poets shun vampires
actually
mixed well with
palm-readers named sister maria
not the phone sex astrologers
poets frequent cyberspace
coffee houses
pass around the phoenix riddle
consult bhavagad-gita again
shave their heads
Hare Hare. Hare Krishna
at the patrick henry mall

Bitches, all of 'em sniffs
a stiff Ezra
travelling the Appian Way
browning in his hip pocket
while Li Po plays the handkerchief
meanwhile Icarus ditched
the wings
but not before our brittle hearts
stirred
for a bird

amateur night at the Apollo

the boy doing luther vandross's
rendition of Dionne Warwick before
the cascade of catcalls

doesn't faze the girl
in the blue cocktail dress
that doesn't look the way it did
in the store in Dallas

"'and I'm telling you, I ain't goin,'
you know, the song that Jennifer Holiday sang."
A warbling vibrato good enough
for Ebenezer Baptist
    doesn't have a prayer
                  in Harlem

next up
the man whose adam's apple
is a mercury ball in a
neurotic thermometer
doo wop finger popping
employed in the service
of conjuring some old school

quicker than you can say,
"a house is not a home"
the coon clown who waits
in the wings

scoots to sweep away
the one whose sweat didn't
turn to gold
after adjusting
the microphone
next up-

Geraldine's rules of order:

a.   if you're not up to being
       human
       make a visual statement

b.   you deserve some peace of mind
       you don't have to ask god for

c.   so god likes your fandance
       he'll play it back
       and freeze-frame it
       call it history

d.   I play back mel blanc cartoons
       because I know you can
       fake a facsimile
       and I'll gladly pay you
       Tuesday

a dog's life

(Bow wow wow yippie yo yippi eee)
Buster's not satisfied to eat his
puppy chow
he wants to lick
the lotion off women's legs
he wants to do more than sniff
baby's ice cream
although his own food is
adequate to his needs
it is not sweet
and Buster wants something sweet
       after all
  he lives an unnuetered
         dog's life—
           and will Buster master
the right
bitch
       the one
that'll make his
            ears stand straight up
as they do
   when they pick up
the first flutter trills
of Jean Luc Ponty's
wild violin

Woooo Wooo Wooo
his eyes go round and sideways

   badboybuster
dreams in the kennel
       thinking all this stuff over
while he licks his doghood

from one music lover to another

when you turn up the bass too loud
the door vibrates
neighbors know you're
inside
trying your best
to get off
to everybody from
brubeck to basie to bonnie raitt

the door vibrates
and your heart
beats for the good note
the one that will somehow last
beyond your concrete steps
with the geranium plants
that you have not watered since
the last rain
tears won't do-
salty and too few
must have clean water not
soiled by
the deadly seven
must have clean water
if not from you then
wherever the idea
of god has taken up residence

up there in the sky somewhere

birds flap their wings
at so many somethings per second
music alone cannot suffice
must have something else
since you abandoned camus
and sex
you are alive still
in a universe
where celie could not even reach god
to tell him she was good

Declaratives

the ghost of jimi hendrix presides
over an indifferent desert
"the wind screams, 'Mary' down
down down
night's bloody history mystery
scud missiles murder metaphor
in primetime
milton's dissembling frog has multiplied
his grief as world leaders
flanking god
speak in sync
their mouths dripping oil
crabs miss the moon's debut
don't know backwards from sideways
each one an intifada
proud mary asks
what's love got to do with it
urban alchemists consider ways and means
of surviving a fin de siecle they
cannot change.

Southland

*". . .in the land of cotton
old times there
are not forgotten
look away . . ."*

Booker T son of ole virginy
wanders around in the coal mine
he is afraid   (sinner, please don't let this harvest pass)
he is looking for a podium
a hoe and a match
a match a hoe and a podium
gotta got to gotta
school invisible (wo)men on
how to game their
way into the academy in
one long stroke
                    (pause here for minstrel interlude)
imagine there's no heaven
just melting clocks
on barren fields that ragtime Toomer
willed to Gurdjieff or ragtime Gurdjieff willed to Toomer

Passing Little Buckland,
I think I spy him in the cottonfield
("Booker, is that you?")
practicing how he will say

"O Lawd, de cotton am so grassy,
de work am so hard, and the sun am so hot
dat I b'lieve dis darky am called to preach!"

the magic words for makin and unmakin
"most black, brother, most black"
Off to see the Wizard
I turn off the highway
and there he is
behind the shotgun house in
block-back coat and stetson hat
helping Trueblood get his lie straight:

Wizard: Now when they ask you were you there,
             what are you going to say?
Young man: Wasn't me, man. And I wasn't there, but
             sometimes it causes me to
             tremble, tremble, tremble.
Wizard: That won't do. Won't do.
Young man: Then what I'm sposed ta say, Chief?
Wizard: "I have not been successful in securing any
             information that would throw any accurate
             light..."

but DuBois interrupts
from the porch to grouse about fractions.
He told us that we were divided
against ourselves.
He resolved his issues in Ghana,
Meanwhile, a.d. (After Du Bois)
we marched on and on
Washington
D.C.

Somebody's playin Gershwin so sweetly.
"It ain't necessarily so and so

I catch my mouth disappearing
as an involuntary "yassuh" slips out **hisssssss**
to caress
some distinct dude
who volunteers to split history's tab.
       I demure.

Says he: "What we have is a failure to communicate"
Says I: "We can't all get along,"
but sweetly, in the key of
"Roll Jordan, Roll/ Roll Jordan Roll/ I want
to go to heaven when I die/ to see old Jordan roll
over.

Sometimes I (dis)remember things, too.
Lincoln Perry played Stepin Fetchit
Jesse B. Semple played himself
                     "*Do nothing till you hear from me*"

Gershwin was making some headway,
but he dissolved into some
Monkish stuff with piano, saxophone, and bass.

"The day the music died" posthaste
they had not consulted me and some bluesprints.
They were singing
"bye bye miss american pie"
I could have told them that Elvis is not dead yet
but I couldn't catch rye on the levee with the boys
My sisters advised me to imbibe
heavy doses of oliver lake nina simone k.d. lang aretha miles
dvorak

then find a brother or sister who could help me
come
       to
              terms

my brother thinks

I have rubbed my head
against the Jericho walls of

                                   (drums)

edu(my)cation for so long/ for so long/for so long
that I have
mis-termed the struggle
       my mind a blackbo(a)rd
                with inscription
(Take me to da water, or
       take me tu da wadder, or
                tek me ta da wata ohyesohyes)
consider Mr. Brown's sterling decoding
system
to determine
wich one is correc'
Little neo/colored girls still lament
nappy edges
though dark and lovely can burn
all trace of africa
from the temple
leaving shiny bald skin in its place
Is it,
"Who be ye?"
or
"Who you be?"

The answer lay festering in a (w)hole
note knotted until
it showed up unannounced
on the mid-Atlantic shore,
then, resurfaced in New England pews
or exquisite South Carolina grill work.
News of this marvel travelled
by way of Jacob's ladder

                        (every round goes higher, higher)

The answer waded in the water.
pushed through a hole
till it was worn into itself.
The answer swam to shore with Shine
    (whose light is a-comin).
Coltrane blows sweetly over the Carolinas
supreme love.

How we be.
We be   *(you can play dixie right here)*
Do we be
We be   *(play john lee hooker here)*
Do we be
We be   *(play billie and mamie and bessie)*
Do we be   *(play coltrane and pharoah and
                                  the sonny's)*
we be . . . we be . . . we be . . . we be . . .
webewebewebewebewebewebe –

                                      (drums)

28 degrees on channel 13

it's 28 degrees in houston tonight
sanchez scrambles for cover
to his cardboard box/haven
under the pierce elevated
he thanks god
he's alive

i'm thinking about stoic christian thanking
i'm thinking to thank for
thinking
there I go
again—
stuttering
just like Jesus or—
jacks
when the ball
bouncing off pavement
turns in the air
while the other hand
picks up the ones, then twos

just like
people
hardest to pierce the paved parts of
the ones
       then one
I love or one I hate one
I regret or one I envy

the biggest hurdle
the y in I

thought blinks at its self-
generating
chasms the
gaps will
  get
    you

back to sanchez

who can be grateful for
the simplest things
a cardboard box?
no.

breath
his soul's engine closing the
winds gaps its rages

in the cavern beneath
the pierce elevated his
mind/heart fills the idle spaces
sanchez' heat draws all the heat from
rage making his heart normal
blood circulates free
ly mo-men-tari-ly
nogapshere

From Beaumont to Benin

*This is a 16th A.D. century bronze plaque showing
a stylised human figure with a head, hands,
and legs, said to represent the messenger of death.*
H. 47 cm. National Museum, Benin City.

Miss Lily has been living across the street since
before this house was built. She says,
"before the colored came,"
(as if vitiligo had made her different)
           "dogwood trees usedta grow here, that's all."
Willi and Nadine believe
she is older than god.

Her legs are spider's legs and
she doesn't blink
behind her glasses.
Nadine and Willi believe
she has eyes
in the back of her head.
She has no children
calls her cats her "babies,"
and scolds them when they soil
the porcelain and plastic dolls
that sit upright all over the house.
The cats never leave the house.

But Miss Lily goes out
for funerals. She says,
"One must pay one's respects
to the dead."

She goes at least once a week
sometimes three times
during the winter season
her spotted hands pressed in prayer
for those who've passed
and those who will pass.

Miss Lily doesn't wear perfume,
"because," she says, she
"likes the smell of the living body."
She has never married.

Texas Poem
(for Leah)

"Mama, don't let the sun bite me
Sun bite me"
she cries and shields her eyes
with innocent arms
and the sun
    the sun stares
with the third eye of a madman
and the land lies low
    to the ground
errant squirrels, dogs and cats who
mis-calculated stiffen and bloat
    on the highway
mid-afternoon
"Mama, clouds hide"
clouds disperse, daughter

    thieves thinned out to cigarette smoke bereft of will
  caught in the grim heat
of conspiracy
  they vanish
        in dust and
chickweed
the sun though
  the sun has not moved

Nina or somethin like happy
Nashville, 1962

wiry little black woman
with a great big mouth
sends gravelly songs to our nerve
endings
sky opens up
offers to hold us

Trouble in mind, I'm blue,
but I won't be blue always,
cuz the sun's gonna shine
in my backdoor some day

Mama would turn on Nina's
scratched record and sit down
after she and daddy had been
drinking and screaming
exercising blues
two prairie chickens
on unholy dancing ground
in the living room, dining room
kitchen, front porch
and she would cry
mama would
trouble in mind
as if that skinny black woman
on that spinning vinyl circle
had stepped up on mama's porch

and sat down with her
on her living room couch
and you could stand up and
shout
or sit down and
shout

and didn't nothin matter
no more except that woman's
serious contralto
that dipped in low notes
and laid claim to edgy riffs
and sometimes high notes
as if to say
ain't nobody's business

yes
and it was Nashville, but
Mississippi Goddamn that too
I didn't need to rest my head
on Mama's nervous lap
I knew that she would get
back to herself
cigarette by cigarette
note by note
in Nina's healing mouth

She called herself "Nina,"
little North Carolina gal
like Mama

grandmas rocking on evening porches
humming rhythm songs with no tune
except the one tongue's memory
eased out
of red clay
and Atlantic City longing

we'd sit in the room till
it was lit by steel lamps
outside

My child's heart etched
'why' in oblique ways—
mute shoulders
only Nina would answer
and let the 2:19 train
ease my troubled mind
yes I will
yes I will

Mama: 5'6, 97 lbs, lapsed
music major,
little North Carolina gal
teacher, chain smoker
teacher's daughter
who was the daughter of a teacher:
Mary Corpier had taught the blind
to see anyway
Mama and Daddy
reached for each other
(with murderous hands
two blind minds)

in her own house
playing foul
Hagar's ill-adapted daughter
replays some maudlin Gershwin
trouble is a man and
a good one is hard to find
man trouble in mind
I is your woman now
I is I is

A presbyterian father had etched
redemption
in stripes on her back
she would sleepwalk
in the evenin by the moonlight
married a savior who favored
the father
with back door bluesitis

we would sit
mama and me
stuck in a black vinyl moon's
parabola
rocking back
rocking back
rocking back
to reason
or something like it

***Mary Corpier was principal of a school for the blind in Nashville during the early part of the twentieth century*

Daddy Poem

I.

Got my first diary
in the fifth grade.
Nadine and Coop asked Daddy
for fishing poles.
They wanted to stand,
gap-legged on the bank with him
and cast their lines out
onto the river.

Then, Daddy's lean face was clean
of extraneous flesh,
his cheeks dark blades
unresponsive to child's whim
or wife's advice.
His widow's peak
would fulfill prophecy
when Mama died
before he.

Got his hands
from Papa Johnny,
a sometime carpenter
and gardener year-round.

II.

Papa Johnny's green-tipped
earth-dipped
fingers grasp the chair arms
in anticipation
of the effort to rise,

"Don't need no help, go'n now,"
while holding his son's arm.

When he was willing and able,
no matter the season
there was some green
blooming thing
around Papa's house
He had to midwife
earth's infinite birthing.

Papa Johnny will be
around here forever.
If you don't believe me,
just wait for
the double birth
of his chrysanthemums —
loud yellow in Spring
and brazen orange
in late Fall
when the grass is
indifferent even
to gray.

III.

Beaumont's son didn't plan
to press the flesh of his hands
against wood and steel
or strain his back
to hold high mass
for tomatoes
and green beans.

Daddy's hands delve into
the mystery of flesh
a healer
whose own heart
will not suffer meddlers
poets, wizards, preachers –

"Anybody can do an appendectomy,
if everything goes well.
But what if it doesn't?
Call the doctor and then God,
in that order."

IV.

Mama,
Daddy's ooh blah dee woman —
"Yo mama's from
the land of ooh blah dee,
she's got three eyes,
three eyes for me"

Mama: jesus christ come again on
c(olored) p(eople's) time
your trinity, the golden triangle:
Beaumont, Orange, Port Arthur
"Ooh blah dee, my a-square-suss"
I loved you once
but indifference murders
love's logic
drink by drink

V.

When the world's crud
seeps too deep
into the soil
of his flesh
daddy goes fishin',
casts his line out in the air
on the river.

Daddy dips his hands
into the failing flesh.
Bids sick folks to rise up.

"A black man does what he can,
does what he can, daughter"

VI.
I'm clumsy with sharp things,
but I carry blades in my cheeks,
legacy of father's fathers
mothering

Daddy casts his line outward
on the Cumberland River.

Don't care to dangle
treacherous opportunities
before crappy or bream
who mean only
to go on living
        no fancy bait
no floaters
no 5 lb test lines
to buy bragging rights to
30 lb widemouth bass.

"Baby, a fish can make you look like a damn fool."

I cast my line out
in another order
that moves

from my inside out
into a noisy world,
perhaps to move it.
words
like spider's lines
more tentative than hemp

but nevertheless
edifice
built from the inside
where words leap
like fish
from memory's river
out
swinging like the Count
or simply standing
for something.
Sunlight
on blue-lined
paper.

indigo bunting

as we watched from inside
we heard
the record skip twice
in the next room
then settle in
needle hiss prelude to
gloria lynne's velvet:
and if you could see me too
there would be nothin tragic
in all my dreams of you

rosie starts out walking
toes pointed toward home
but the rain of licks is too much
and then she's
running as if
for life

I see your face

rain sticks to his face
like sweat
as he yanks his belt buckle
rainshiny fingers slip off
the metal

we stand at the window
peeking through the slats
she's late getting home again

rosie stretches her neck as if
she were catching rain
on her tongue
"daddy . . . but I . . ."
and rain assaults his
open mouth
"no . . .
child of mine . . .
stand still, I say . . ."

his belted fist makes
a wilted salute to his tardy daughter
the slap of wet leather sings
on soaked flesh
no "oh, daddy please!"

father

it's falling like wrath
it's falling like vengeance
bending skinny trees,
washing mud and pollen
down suburban sewage drains
making things new
again

I can see how fair you are

each foot indicts passive pavement
run, rosie
I close my eyes and
there you are/ always

in the wash of water
you can't hear his voice
you can't read his lips
like he's chewing rain

he chastises his indigo bunting
she opens her brown mouth to
say sweet-sweet, see-it, see-it
she's late getting home again

the last lick burns

and if you could see me too
too too too too
see it
the needle's stuck again
and you know she tastes salt
in her mouth
not rain

for leah
b. September 29, 1978

I.

a
peace
    rose
sang through our flesh
in a tiny texas winter
don and hermine had known
'78 in transit
but by September
school was in
says you:
here I am
and so you were
there
for us
her airness
new world
daughter
the hip/s
to the hop

*Mrs. Loretta Dolores Broadus Harris
in a photograph taken at the
Club De Lise in Chicago
in the early 1930s.*

Mama Yetta

When I recited my first poem for you, "Mother to Son," "life for me ain't been no crystal stair," you sucked your false teeth and laughed, asking me, "What does a child like you know about hard knocks, much less crystal stairs!" So, now in the light of the missing moon, after the ten o'clock news, when everything's been said and done for one day, I think of your frizzy-fried gray hair and your forever moist lips perched to give every chick and child in Beeville, Texas advice on anything from how to save a marriage to how not to make rice stick to the bottom of the pot.

I know it is your spirit that sweetens or salts the pots, that watches the doings in Beeville, Orange, Texas and Opelousas, Louisiana, your old stompin grounds. *Àshe!*[1] It was you that met me in the clearing, leaped into my heart.

All the while Papa trudged to work, to Greenlea's Grocer Supply early in the morning before the sun woke, all the while Papa trudged down the road with his meek brown paper bag lunch, you and Pancho Villa were scanning the US-Mexico border on the lookout for marauders of the plains, especially if those marauders had soiled your bedsheets the night before. How could I know history lived again right in your kitchen! I was a foolish girl, half listening. I never lied. History was what people did a long time ago. Wasn't it?

I would roll my eyes when you shook your fat finger at

me, sashaying around that sun-bright room while you worried over the gumbo or stuffed an unsuspecting roast—you could always do anything you wanted with meat, make it fall off the bone if you pleased, glad to melt in anybody's mouth who dared, who cared come and sit in your blazing kitchen and talk about things in this world and the next.

How could I forget that you, a Louisiana-born woman, had a mama who rocked her to sleep with stories of Marie Laveau, queen of hoodoo, and all the spirits she conjured to answer her when she called. And did *you* know, as you massaged my head with Royal Crown and fashioned fantastic cornrows, that you, a little woman with wide hips, were bequeathing to me the spirits of land, air, and sea that you had come to know just by being one of God's favorite children? You, Mama Yetta, were tryin to bequeath to me the secrets of the "ere, the oka olushere, the ekolo, the lakoshe, and the akoko." [2]

And the last thing you said to me as you lay there in the hospital, your eyes bereft of clarity (your voice thinned by many winters), but still trying to tell me stuff you had told me all my life —

"Girl, keep your business to ya self, and don't let nobody tell ya about ya family, cause if they comin to ya that way, chere, they don't have no good news."

My tears fell on your parched cheeks. You had always told me that the Louisiana Pipkin girls were known for their butter-soft skin, their shrewd eyes, their generous hearts. You always bragged on your mother's skin but not your own.

"Believe in yourself, because you are of my blood. You come from the lily white Donatta's from across the Sabine River and the ebony Braudus's of Taborian, Mississippi, so be proud and draw on your strength, Lord knows you're stubborn enough, but don't be scared to give your strength and your love to the people. Give it away. Believe in who we were and who you will become, because finally, because finally that's all you got."

How could I know you loved me so, even when you slapped me for impudence ("Girl, don't you backtalk me and pick those dirty drawers up off the floor"), scolded me for not knowing how to set a proper table. "Girl, don't grow up to be no slovenly woman," you'd say, shaking that finger at me, as if you were directing the "New World Symphony."

Mama Yetta, I sit at your old writing desk to conjure you. I sit here as silence and desire kindle memory. Dressed in spirit clothes, you visit me, going so far as to comment on the decor and the disarray of my house. "New towels and lavendar sachet is what you really need, chere, your linen closet should smell fresh."

In your last year, you visited me here once before you went back to the hospital for the last time. You came and drank all of my sparkling water, most of my Heineken—"sure tastes sweet, pour me some more of this, chere"— and commiserated with my next-door neighbor who came over to tell us that she was home on-leave from the downtown hospital. The doctor had told her to go home and practice being with her family, but she wouldn't. Said she couldn't even stand practicing loving them, despite the anti-anxiety medication her psychotherapist gave her, the antibiotics her gynecologist gave her, and the blood pressure pills her internist prescribed. When she left, you warned, me, "Watch that one, 'cause she needs more help than those doctors can think to give her. How many degrees does it take to figure out a woman's broken in body and spirit?"

Yetta, your loving me was a trial by fire. Who spanks

a child, then demands to be kissed—"Kiss your grandmother, chere, or walk out that door and pull another switch off that tree, yes! Honor thy father and thy mother and thy Mama Yetta, too." You gave me all you had and were, whether I wanted it or not. You believed yourself a daughter of Hagar. I know you to be Ochun's child. Spread peace and quiet over me like the warm salt water of the Texas Gulf, and I know I'll be all right in time to come.

Talk to you when I need your gumballs of wisdom, because I know you will come. Mama Yetta Yetta Yetta Yetta — I say your name four times, because the Dogon people say that is the woman's number, and who knows? Maybe you and Pancho Villa and Ochun and the Dogon folks are right, and maybe I'll just keep persevering, 'cause I can't do nothin but. This is your granddaughter talkin, the one who peed the bed and didn't walk till twelve and a half months, the one who was left-handed and stuttered with strangers, the one who rolled her eyes until they crossed one day, the one who loves you still. Goodnight, Mama Yetta. Always remind me of the secrets of *the ere, the oka olushere, the ekolo, the lakoshe, and the akoko,* whenever I start singing dirges and complaining that life for me ain't been no crystal stair.

---

[1] According to Yoruban mythology, "ashe" is the "power to make things happen.

[2] According to Yoruban mythology the ere, oka olushere, ekolo, lakoshe, and the akoko are the messengers by which Olorun sends "ashe."

Other 1999 titles from WINGS PRESS

Poesía Tejana Prize recipients:

Smolt by Nicole Pollentier
    (0-930324-43-9)
Cande, te estoy llamando by Celeste Guzmán
    (0-930324-44-7)
Peace in the Corazón by Victoria García-Zapata
    (0-930324-46-3)
Long Story Short by Mary Grace Rodríguez
    (0-930324-45-5)

Other poetry:

Sonnets to Human Beings by Carmen Tafolla
    (0-930324-47-1)
Garabato Poems by Virgil Suárez
    (0-930324-38-2)
Seven Cigarette Story by Courtenay Martin
    (0-930324-42-0)
Winter Poems from Eagle Pond by Donald Hall
    (0-930324-40-4) Trade ed.
    (0-930324-41-2) Limited/signed

Scholarly:

Biblical Hebrew: An Analytical Introduction
    by Dr. Winfred Lehmann, Dr. Esther Raizen,
    and Dr. H.J.J. Hewitt (0-930324-37-4)

On-line catalogue and ordering:
www.wingspress.com

Colophon

Seven hundred copies of *Mama Yetta and Other Poems*, by Hermine Pinson, have been printed on 70 pound Nekoosa Linen natural paper, containing fifty percent recycled fiber, by Williams Printing & Graphics of San Antonio, Texas. The text was set in 12 point Garamond 3 type. *Mama Yetta and Other Poems* was entirely designed and produced by Bryce Milligan, publisher, Wings Press.

Wings Press was founded in 1975 by J. Whitebird and Joseph F. Lomax as "an informal association of artists and cultural mythologists dedicated to the preservation of the literature of the nation of Texas." The publisher/editor since 1995, Bryce Milligan, is honored to carry on and expand that mission to include the finest in American writing.